More *Easy* Stories Plus

Readings and Activities for Language Skills

Ann Gianola

Instructor, San Diego Community College District
San Diego, California

New Readers Press

More Easy Stories Plus: Readings and Activities for Language Skills
ISBN 978-1-56420-550-6

Copyright © 2005 New Readers Press
New Readers Press
A Publishing Division of ProLiteracy
1320 Jamesville Avenue, Syracuse, New York 13210
www.newreaderspress.com

Printed in the United States of America
9 8 7 6 5 4 3

All proceeds from the sale of New Readers Press materials
support literacy programs in the United States and worldwide.

Acquisitions Editor: Paula L. Schlusberg
Content Editor: Terrie Lipke
Production Manager: Andrea Woodbury
Illustrations: Linda Tiff
Production Specialist: Jeffrey R. Smith
Cover Design: Kimbrly Koennecke

Contents

An Honest Man

Daniel is at a restaurant. He is having lunch alone. He feels something on the floor near his foot. Daniel looks under the table. There is a wallet with $120 and a credit card inside. Daniel looks for identification. He finds a driver's license. The address is near the restaurant.

Daniel eats his lunch and leaves the restaurant. He walks down the street, finds the house, and knocks at the door. A beautiful woman opens the door. "May I speak to Laura?" asks Daniel.

"I am Laura," she answers.

Daniel gives her the wallet. He says, "I found your wallet at the restaurant."

Laura is very happy. She opens the wallet. All of her money is there.

"Thank you very much!" she says. "May I give you a $40 reward?"

"No," says Daniel. "Don't worry about it. It's your money."

"You are a very honest man! I want to do something for you. Please let me take you to lunch tomorrow," says Laura.

"OK," says Daniel. "How about 12:00?"

"Fine," says Laura. "But I'm paying."

Check *yes* or *no.*

Yes   No

1. Daniel is having lunch with his mother.

2. He feels something on the floor.

3. There is $12 inside the wallet.

4. Daniel finds a driver's license.

5. The address is near the restaurant.

6. Daniel gives Laura the wallet.

7. All of her money is gone.

8. Daniel wants the $40 reward.

9. Daniel is an honest man.

▎▎■ Complete each sentence.

address	honest	lunch	wallet
floor	license	reward	worry

1. There is something on the _____ near my foot.

2. Look and see if there is a driver's _____ inside.

3. Is this _____ near the restaurant?

4. There is a lot of money in this _____.

5. May I give you a $40 _____?

6. Don't _____ about it. It's your money.

7. Thank you. You are a very _____ man.

8. I want to take you to _____ tomorrow at 12:00.

▎▎■ Match the opposites.

____ 1. find   a. none

____ 2. near   b. dishonest

____ 3. honest   c. together

____ 4. all   d. ugly

____ 5. alone   e. far from

____ 6. beautiful   f. lose

■■ Match the words and pictures.

credit card	identification	money

_____   _____   _____

■■ Returning the Wallet

Practice the dialog with a partner.

May I speak to Laura?

I am Laura.

I found your wallet at the restaurant.

Thank you very much!

I am happy to return it.

May I give you a reward?

No, it's your money. Don't worry about it.

May I take you to lunch tomorrow at noon?

That sounds great. See you then.

▮▮▮ Check the correct picture.

1.
_____ _____

3.
_____ _____

2.
_____ _____

4.
_____ _____

▮▮▮ Check the items in your wallet.

**Put a check next to the things you keep in your wallet.
Write other things in your wallet on the lines below.**

____ driver's license   ____ medical information

____ cash   ____ coins

____ credit card   ____ photos

____ health insurance card   ____ store coupons

____ receipts   ____ library card

_____   _____

▎▎■ What about you?

Circle *yes* or *no.* Then write questions and ask your partner.

Yes **No** **1.** I look for identification when I find a wallet.

Do you look for identification when you find a wallet?
_____

Yes **No** **2.** I return things I find.

_____

Yes **No** **3.** I would take a $40 reward.

_____

Yes **No** **4.** I think Daniel is honest.

_____

Yes **No** **5.** I think Daniel needs to pay for lunch.

_____

▎■■ Topics for Discussion or Writing

1. What are some other things you find? What do you do after you find them?

2. How can you help return a wallet to someone?

3. For what reasons can you give or receive a reward?

Confusing Internet

Emma is at home. She is thinking about her sister Clara in Germany. She looks at her watch. She wants to call Clara now, but she can't. It's very late in Germany. Clara is probably sleeping.

Emma's son Hans says, "Send Aunt Clara an e-mail." But Emma doesn't like the computer. She thinks the Internet is very confusing. Hans tells his mother that e-mail is fast and easy. "You need to try it. It is fantastic."

Emma shakes her head. "No," she says. "I like the telephone. I never want to touch the computer again."

Hans sits down at the computer. He gets on the Internet and checks his e-mail. "Here is a message from Aunt Clara," says Hans. "She wants you to visit her in Germany this summer. Open the telephone book. Look for a travel agent, and buy a ticket."

Emma sits in a chair next to Hans. "I have a better idea," she says. "Let's look for a cheaper ticket on the Internet."

■■ Check *yes* or *no.*

Yes **No**

1. Emma is at home.

2. She is thinking about her brother in Germany.

3. She calls Clara in Germany.

4. Hans tells his mother to send an e-mail.

5. Emma likes the computer.

6. Emma thinks the Internet is fast and easy.

7. Hans sits down at the computer.

8. There is a message from Aunt Clara.

9. Clara wants Emma to visit this summer.

10. Emma looks for a travel agent in the telephone book.

What is the category?

aunt	Internet	mother	son
e-mail	letter	newspaper	telephone
fax	library	sister	telephone book

Family Members	Types of Communication	Places to Look for Information
1. _____	1. _____	1. _____
2. _____	2. _____	2. _____
3. _____	3. _____	3. _____
4. _____	4. _____	4. _____

Match the meanings.

_____ 1. computer

_____ 2. summer

_____ 3. cheaper

_____ 4. visit

_____ 5. ticket

_____ 6. touch

_____ 7. confusing

a. warm season after spring

b. put your hand on something

c. electronic machine that stores information

d. hard to understand

e. paper you get when you travel

f. costs less money

g. go and see

▪▪▪ Complete each sentence.

better	look for	probably	visit
Internet	message	sits down	

1. It is late in Germany. Clara is _____ sleeping.

2. Hans _____ at the computer.

3. There is a _____ from Aunt Clara.

4. She wants Emma to _____ this summer.

5. Hans tells his mother to _____ a travel agent.

6. His mother has a _____ idea.

7. They look for a cheaper ticket on the _____.

▪▪▪ Together at the Computer

Practice the dialog with a partner.

Flight #253

Can you help me plan my trip?

When do you want to leave?

I want to leave for Germany on July 11th and return home on August 3rd.

Here's a round-trip flight for only $800.

That's a great price!

I agree. Let's get the credit card.

Check the correct picture.

1.
____ ____

3.
____ ____

2.
____ ____

4.
____ ____

Check the good ideas.

How can you use the Internet to plan a trip? Put a check next to the good ideas. Write other ideas on the lines below.

____ buy airline tickets

____ call your sister

____ look for restaurants

____ find a travel agent

____ pack your suitcase

____ find hotels

____ get a nice taxi driver

____ get a weather report

____ get maps and directions

____ ask your boss for time off

_____   _____

■■■ What about you?

Circle *yes* or *no*. Then write questions and ask your partner.

Yes   No   1. I have a computer at home.

   Do you have a computer at home?

Yes   No   2. I use the Internet at home.

_____

Yes   No   3. I send e-mail sometimes.

_____

Yes   No   4. I think the Internet is confusing.

_____

Yes   No   5. I think the Internet is fast and easy.

_____

■■■ Topics for Discussion or Writing

1. Where does your family live? Is there a time difference between you and your family? If so, how many hours? How do you communicate with your family?

2. Do you use the Internet? If so, what do you use it for?

3. What are some things you can buy on the Internet?

Rainy Weather

Leo lives in Seattle, Washington. Seattle is a beautiful city. Leo has a good job and many friends. But there is one problem. It rains a lot in Seattle, especially in the winter. Leo doesn't like rainy weather. He doesn't like wet clothes. He doesn't like wet shoes. He doesn't like carrying an umbrella everywhere.

In September, Leo has time for a two-week vacation. He wants to go somewhere warm and dry. Leo decides to go to Cancun, in southern Mexico. It has good weather and pretty beaches. Leo is very excited.

The day before Leo leaves, it is sunny. Leo is running in the park. He sees his friend Enrique. Enrique is from Mexico. Leo says, "I leave tomorrow. I can't wait!"

"Have a great trip," says Enrique. "What are you taking?"

"Very little," answers Leo. "I'm just taking T-shirts, shorts, and sandals."

"Don't forget an umbrella," says Enrique. "In Cancun, this is the rainy season."

Check *yes* or *no*.

Yes **No**

____	____	**1.** Leo lives in Cancun.
____	____	**2.** Leo has a good job and many friends.
____	____	**3.** It rains a lot in Seattle.
____	____	**4.** Leo likes carrying an umbrella everywhere.
____	____	**5.** He wants to go somewhere warm and dry.
____	____	**6.** Leo decides to go to Cancun.
____	____	**7.** Leo is running in the park the day before he leaves.
____	____	**8.** His friend Enrique is from Seattle.
____	____	**9.** This is the dry season in Cancun.

▪■■ What is the category?

dry	rainy	spring	T-shirt
fall	sandals	summer	warm
hat	shorts	sunny	winter

Weather Words

1. _____

2. _____

3. _____

4. _____

Four Seasons

1. _____

2. _____

3. _____

4. _____

Clothes for Warm Weather

1. _____

2. _____

3. _____

4. _____

▪■■ Match the meanings.

____ 1. job

____ 2. umbrella

____ 3. city

____ 4. vacation

____ 5. friend

____ 6. beach

a. someone you like very much

b. work you do for money

c. a time away from work

d. something to protect you from the rain

e. sandy area next to the ocean

f. a place where people live and work

▪▪▪ Complete the story.

happy	many	southern	vacation
lives	season	take	weather

Enrique _____ in Seattle. It rains a lot in Seattle,

but Enrique is very _____. He has a good job and

_____ friends. His friend Leo is going on a

_____ to Cancun. It is in _____ Mexico.

Enrique is from Mexico. He knows about the _____.

He tells Leo to _____ an umbrella. It is the rainy

_____ in Cancun.

▪▪▪ Talking in the Park

Practice the dialog with a partner.

What a beautiful day!

Yes, I love this time of the year.

When do you leave on your trip?

I leave tomorrow. I can't wait!

Are you taking an umbrella?

Of course not! I'm going to Cancun!

Yes, but this is the rainy season.

Check the correct picture.

1.
_____ _____

3.
_____ _____

2.
_____ _____

4.
_____ _____

Check the things to pack.

What do you take on vacation? Put a check next to the things you pack. Write other things on the lines below.

____ a hat

____ pants

____ a camera

____ shorts

____ a bathing suit

____ sunscreen

____ an umbrella

____ medicine

____ a heavy coat

____ sandals

_____

_____

▌▌▌ What about you?

Circle *yes* or *no.* Then write questions and ask your partner.

Yes **No** **1.** I live in a city where it rains a lot.

Do you live in a city where it rains a lot?

Yes **No** **2.** I like rainy weather.

_____

Yes **No** **3.** I carry an umbrella everywhere.

_____

Yes **No** **4.** I take an umbrella on vacation.

_____

Yes **No** **5.** I take vacations in the summer.

_____

▌▌▌ Topics for Discussion or Writing

1. How is the weather where you live? How is it in your native country? Describe the seasons in each place.

2. What kind of clothes do you need for rainy weather?

3. Do you have many friends? Are your friends from other countries?

Spicy Food

Colin and his wife are at an Indian restaurant. Colin likes Indian food. It is spicy and delicious. The House of India is his favorite restaurant. Colin and his wife look at the menu. Soon the waiter comes to take their order. Colin says, "Chicken curry, please. And I would like it extra hot."

Colin's wife doesn't like spicy food. She says, "The same for me, but not spicy. I want it very mild."

In a few minutes the waiter brings their plates. They pick up their forks and taste the chicken curry. Colin says, "The food isn't very spicy tonight."

Colin's wife looks surprised. Tears are coming out of her eyes. She grabs her water and drinks it all.

"Colin!" she cries. "This is your dinner!"

Colin feels sorry. He trades plates with his wife. Colin asks the waiter for more water. He gives his wife a napkin to wipe her eyes. "Sorry, dear," he says. "Next week we can go to your favorite Mexican restaurant."

▪ ▪ Check *yes* or *no.*

Yes **No**

____ ____ **1.** Colin and his wife are at a Mexican restaurant.

____ ____ **2.** Colin likes Indian food.

____ ____ **3.** Soon the doctor comes to take his order.

____ ____ **4.** Colin wants his chicken curry extra hot.

____ ____ **5.** Colin's wife likes spicy food.

____ ____ **6.** In a few minutes the waiter brings their plates.

____ ____ **7.** Colin says that his food is very mild.

____ ____ **8.** Colin's wife drinks all her water.

____ ____ **9.** Colin gives her a napkin to wipe her mouth.

____ ____ **10.** Next week they can go back to the House of India.

▮▮▮ What is the category?

Chinese	glass	Italian	napkin
delicious	hot	Mexican	plate
fork	Indian	mild	spicy

How Food Tastes	**Things on a Table**	**Types of Restaurants**
1. _____	1. _____	1. _____
2. _____	2. _____	2. _____
3. _____	3. _____	3. _____
4. _____	4. _____	4. _____

▮▮▮ Match the meanings.

_____ 1. waiter

_____ 2. trade

_____ 3. dinner

_____ 4. tears

_____ 5. menu

_____ 6. favorite

a. the one you like the most

b. liquid that comes from your eyes

c. list of food at a restaurant

d. to exchange

e. afternoon or evening meal

f. person who takes orders and serves food

Underline the word from the story.

1. The House of (India/Mexico) is his favorite restaurant.

2. Soon the waiter comes to take their (order/menu).

3. Colin says, "I would like it extra (mild/hot)."

4. Colin's wife says, "The same for me, but not (spicy/delicious)."

5. They pick up their (plates/forks) and taste the chicken curry.

6. Colin's wife looks (satisfied/surprised).

7. Colin asks for more (waiter/water).

8. He gives his wife a napkin to wipe her (eyes/nose).

Talking to the Waiter

Practice the dialog with a partner.

Excuse me. Waiter?

Is everything all right here?

Not really. You gave my dinner to her.

Oh, I'm so sorry.

Can you bring more water please?

Of course. Right away.

And can we get a few more napkins?

Sure. I'll be right back.

Check the correct picture.

1.
___ ___

3.
___ ___

2.
___ ___

4.
___ ___

Check the good ideas.

There is a problem with your food. What can you do? Put a check next to the good ideas. Write other ideas on the lines below.

____ talk to the waiter   ____ complain to the manager

____ drink a lot of water   ____ go to another restaurant

____ say you're not hungry   ____ put food in the trash

____ leave no tip   ____ throw a napkin at the waiter

____ eat half of it   ____ say it's delicious

_____   _____

▪▫▪ What about you?

Circle *yes* or *no.* Then write questions and ask your partner.

Yes　**No**　**1.** I like spicy food.

Do you like spicy food?

Yes　**No**　**2.** I like extra hot food.

_____

Yes　**No**　**3.** I like mild food.

_____

Yes　**No**　**4.** I think Indian food is delicious.

_____

Yes　**No**　**5.** I think Mexican food is delicious.

_____

▪▫▪ Topics for Discussion or Writing

1. What is your favorite restaurant? Where is it? What kind of food does it serve?

2. What different foods do people in your family like?

3. What can you do when you eat something too hot or spicy?

Parking Ticket

Hal is driving around the parking lot at the bank. He can't find a place to park. Hal sees two parking spaces, but the lines are blue. The spaces are for disabled people. Hal is not disabled.

Hal looks at his watch. He decides to park between the blue lines for a few minutes. Hal enters the bank and fills out a deposit slip for $400. Hal is happy. He likes to save money. He waits in a long line. After 15 minutes, Hal returns to the parking lot. There is a police officer next to Hal's car. He is writing a parking ticket. The officer asks, "Is this your car?"

"Yes," answers Hal. "I can move it now."

"Too late," says the police officer. "This space is for disabled people only. Be more careful next time."

Hal looks at the fee on the ticket. He is very sad. Hal moves his car. Then he goes back into the bank. He fills out a withdrawal slip for $400. Hal needs the money to pay his parking ticket.

▮▮▮ Check *yes* or *no*.

Yes   No

_____ _____ **1.** Hal is driving around the parking lot at the bank.

_____ _____ **2.** He sees three parking spaces.

_____ _____ **3.** Hal is disabled.

_____ _____ **4.** He decides to park between the blue lines for a few minutes.

_____ _____ **5.** Hal fills out a deposit slip for $500.

_____ _____ **6.** He likes to save money.

_____ _____ **7.** A police officer writes Hal a parking ticket.

_____ _____ **8.** The parking space is for disabled people and Hal.

_____ _____ **9.** Hal is very happy about the ticket.

_____ _____ **10.** He fills out a withdrawal slip for $400.

▮▮▮ Underline the word from the story.

1. Hal is driving (around/into) the parking lot.

2. He sees two parking spaces, but the lines are (white/blue).

3. He is not (a driver/disabled).

4. Hal decides to park (between/beside) the blue lines.

5. He enters the bank and fills (out/up) a deposit slip.

6. Hal likes to save (money/time).

7. The police officer asks, "Is this your (wheelchair/car)?"

8. Hal goes back (into/out) the bank.

▮▮▮ Match the meanings.

_____ **1.** disabled

_____ **2.** deposit

_____ **3.** fee

_____ **4.** police officer

_____ **5.** withdraw

_____ **6.** parking lot

a. to take money out of the bank

b. an open area to put your car

c. handicapped

d. to put money into the bank

e. someone who arrests people that break laws

f. money you have to pay

■ ■ ■ Complete the story.

bank	deposit	driving	spaces
car	disabled	mirror	ticket

Ava is disabled. She drives a special _____. There is a

disabled sign on her rearview _____. Today Ava is at the

_____. She wants to _____ some money.

Ava is _____ around the parking lot. She sees two blue

parking _____, but other cars are parked there. One car

does not have a _____ sign. Ava is upset. She wants a

police officer to write that driver a _____.

■ ■ ■ Talking to the Police Officer

Practice the dialog with a partner.

Is this your car, sir?

Yes, it is.

This space is for disabled people only.

OK, Officer. I can move it now.

Sorry, you're too late. Here is your ticket.

Oh, no! Is the fee really $350?

Yes, it is. Next time, be more careful.

▮▮ Write the dollar amount you hear.

1. _____

2. _____

3. _____

4. _____

5. _____

6. _____

7. _____

8. _____

9. _____

10. _____

11. _____

12. _____

▮▮ Check the reasons for tickets.

Put a check next to the reasons people in your native country can get a ticket. Write other reasons people get tickets on the lines below.

____ parking in a disabled space

____ littering

____ speeding

____ driving without a license

____ jaywalking

_____

_____

____ not wearing a seat belt

____ parking in a red zone

____ driving under the influence

____ driving without insurance

____ expired license plates

_____

_____

■ ■ ■ What about you?

Circle *yes* or *no*. Then write questions and ask your partner.

Yes   No   1. I drive to the bank.

Do you drive to the bank?

Yes   No   2. I always find a place to park.

_____

Yes   No   3. I sometimes park in a disabled space.

_____

Yes   No   4. I deposit money in the bank.

_____

Yes   No   5. I withdraw money from the bank.

_____

■ ■ ■ Topics for Discussion or Writing

1. Do you know anyone with a disability? What are some ways you can be disabled?

2. What do you need to do after getting a ticket?

3. Are you trying to save money? Where do you keep your savings? What are you saving money for?

Noisy Neighbor

Vera is a landlady. She owns a small apartment building. Most of the tenants are very quiet, but one person is noisy. His name is Jerry. He lives on the second floor. Jerry likes big parties. He likes loud music and dancing.

Other tenants work in the morning. They need to get up early. At midnight, Mrs. Wing on the first floor is upset. She calls Vera and says, "I can't sleep. That music is driving me crazy." Vera knocks on Jerry's door. Jerry turns down the music. After a few minutes, he turns it up again.

The next day Vera puts a letter in Jerry's mailbox. It says: "Dear Jerry: You're too noisy. You are bothering the other tenants. I have to evict you. You have 30 days to find another place to live."

Jerry reads the letter. Then he calls Vera. "I'm so sorry," says Jerry. "Please don't evict me. Can we talk about this tomorrow? I need to get ready for my party tonight."

■ ■ Check *yes* or *no*.

Yes   No

____ ____   **1.** Vera owns a small apartment building.

____ ____   **2.** Most of the tenants are very noisy.

____ ____   **3.** Jerry lives on the first floor.

____ ____   **4.** Other tenants work in the morning.

____ ____   **5.** Mrs. Wing calls Jerry.

____ ____   **6.** Vera knocks on Jerry's door.

____ ____   **7.** Vera puts a letter on Jerry's table.

____ ____   **8.** Jerry is bothering the other tenants.

____ ____   **9.** Jerry has three days to find another place to live.

____ ____   **10.** Jerry wants to talk about this tomorrow.

■ ■ ■ Complete each sentence.

bothering	landlady	midnight	tenant
evict	letter	party	upset

1. Your loud music is _____ other people.

2. Please put this _____ in his mailbox.

3. It's noisy and she can't sleep. She is very _____.

4. The man on the second floor is having a _____.

5. Call the _____. Her name is Vera.

6. Mrs. Wing is a very quiet _____.

7. I have to _____ you. You must leave in 30 days.

8. It's after _____! People need to get up early.

■ ■ ■ Match the opposites.

____ 1. small   **a.** night

____ 2. quiet   **b.** go to bed

____ 3. get up   **c.** big

____ 4. morning   **d.** late

____ 5. early   **e.** turn up

____ 6. turn down   **f.** noisy

36 Lesson 6

Match the words and pictures.

call	knock	write

_____   _____   _____

No More Loud Parties

Practice the dialog with a partner.

This is the landlady. How can I help you?

I need to talk to you about the tenant upstairs.

Sure. What is it?

He's driving me crazy. I can't sleep at night.

What is he doing?

He's having loud parties all the time.

He can't do that. I need to talk to him.

Thanks. I work early in the morning.

No problem. I understand.

▌▌▐ Check the correct picture.

1.

     _____   _____

3.

     _____   _____

2.

     _____   _____

4.

     _____   _____

▌▐ Check the good ideas.

What can you do about a noisy neighbor? Put a check next to the good ideas. Write other ideas on the lines below.

____ call the landlord   ____ yell at your neighbor

____ play loud music   ____ dance in your apartment

____ talk to your neighbor   ____ call the police

____ wear earplugs   ____ write him a letter

____ go to the parties   ____ bang on the walls

_____   _____

▋▋▋ What about you?

Circle *yes* or *no.* Then write questions and ask your partner.

Yes   **No**   **1.** I live in an apartment building.

Do you live in an apartment building?

Yes   **No**   **2.** I have a noisy neighbor.

_____

Yes   **No**   **3.** I like big parties.

_____

Yes   **No**   **4.** I need to get up early for work.

_____

Yes   **No**   **5.** I call the landlord sometimes.

_____

▋▋▋ Topics for Discussion or Writing

1. Do you have neighbors? Where do they live? Are they quiet or noisy?

2. What kind of noise bothers you at home? What can you do about it?

3. What are some reasons to call the landlord or landlady?

A Funny Message

Yosef works in a busy hotel. He stands at the front desk. He gives information to hotel guests. He makes calls and delivers messages. Yosef starts work at 5:00 A.M. In the afternoon, he is very tired.

At 1:00 P.M., Mrs. Allen from room 671 calls the front desk. She is getting her hair done at the hotel salon. Mrs. Allen says, "My husband is resting now. But please call our room at 2:00. Tell him to meet me for lunch at the Garden Restaurant. And he needs to wear comfortable shoes. Later I want to see the gorillas at the zoo."

Yosef doesn't write down Mrs. Allen's message. He can remember it. He looks at the clock at 2:00. Yosef yawns. He feels very tired. It's time to go home. But first he picks up the phone and calls room 671.

He says, "Good afternoon, Mr. Allen. Your wife is getting her hair done with the gorillas at the zoo. Then she's eating comfortable shoes for lunch in the garden."

Check *yes* or *no*.

Yes　**No**

____ ____ 　**1.** Yosef works in a busy restaurant.

____ ____ 　**2.** Yosef gives information to hotel guests.

____ ____ 　**3.** Yosef starts work at 4:00 A.M.

____ ____ 　**4.** Mrs. Allen calls the front desk at 2:00 P.M.

____ ____ 　**5.** Her husband is eating lunch.

____ ____ 　**6.** Mrs. Allen wants her husband to meet her for lunch.

____ ____ 　**7.** Later Mrs. Allen wants to see the zebras at the zoo.

____ ____ 　**8.** Yosef writes down Mrs. Allen's message.

____ ____ 　**9.** Yosef feels very tired at 2:00.

____ ____ 　**10.** Yosef delivers a funny message to Mr. Allen.

◼◻◼ Complete each sentence.

comfortable	information	remember	resting
getting	message	restaurant	write down

1. Don't call my husband now. He is _____.

2. Do you have _____ shoes? It is a long walk.

3. She is _____ her hair done at 1:00.

4. Is there a _____ in this hotel?

5. I need some _____ about the zoo.

6. I don't _____ the room number. Is it 671 or 761?

7. Will you deliver this _____ to Mr. Allen?

8. Please _____ your telephone number on this paper.

◼◻◼ Match the meanings.

____ **1.** hotel   **a.** a machine that shows the time

____ **2.** husband   **b.** married man

____ **3.** salon   **c.** a place you pay to stay in

____ **4.** tired   **d.** sleepy

____ **5.** guest   **e.** a place to get your hair done

____ **6.** clock   **f.** someone staying in a hotel

▪▪▫ Complete the story.

delivers	funny	hotel	room
front	hair	phone	wife

Mr. Allen is resting in _____ 671. His _____ is

not there. She is at the salon in the _____. She is getting

her _____ done. At 2:00 the _____ rings. Mr.

Allen picks up the phone. It is Yosef at the _____ desk.

Yosef delivers a very _____ message. Mr. Allen

laughs. Then Yosef _____ the right message. Yosef hangs

up the phone. He needs to go home and rest.

▪▪▫ Message for a Guest

Practice the dialog with a partner.

Hello, Mr. Allen. I have a message from
your wife.

What is it?

Please meet her for lunch at 2:00.

Where will she be?

At the Garden Restaurant. It's here in the hotel.

OK. Thanks for the message.

Check the correct picture.

1.
___   ___

3.
___   ___

2.
___   ___

4.
___   ___

Write the time you hear.

1. _____   7. _____

2. _____   8. _____

3. _____   9. _____

4. _____   10. _____

5. _____   11. _____

6. _____   12. _____

■■■ What about you?

Circle *yes* or *no.* Then write questions and ask your partner.

Yes **No** **1.** I make phone calls in English.

Do you make phone calls in English?

Yes **No** **2.** I write down messages in English.

_____

Yes **No** **3.** I deliver messages in English.

_____

Yes **No** **4.** I start work at 5:00 A.M.

_____

Yes **No** **5.** I feel tired in the afternoon.

_____

■■■ Topics for Discussion or Writing

1. Do you have a job? What time do you start work? What time do you go home?

2. Is there a zoo in your community? What animals can you see there?

3. Do you ever say or hear funny things? Give an example.

A Doctor Visit

Anjay rides a bicycle everywhere. He rides to and from work. He rides to the store. He rides to visit his friends. Anjay likes riding his bicycle. He saves money, too. He doesn't pay for gas. He doesn't pollute the air. It is also good exercise. Anjay is very happy with his transportation. He never wants to buy a car.

Sometimes after riding his bicycle, Anjay's knees hurt. Sometimes they hurt a little. Sometimes they hurt a lot. Anjay is worried about his knees. He decides to visit a doctor.

Anjay rides his bicycle to the doctor's office. The doctor examines Anjay's knees for a long time. Then she says, "This is probably not serious. But you have to rest your knees. You need to stop riding your bicycle for a while."

"No," answers Anjay. "That's impossible. I don't want to buy a car."

"I am not telling you to buy a car," says the doctor. "I am telling you to take the bus."

■ ■ ■ Check *yes* or *no*.

Yes   No

____ ____   **1.** Anjay takes the bus everywhere.

____ ____   **2.** Anjay likes riding a bicycle.

____ ____   **3.** He pays a lot of money for gas.

____ ____   **4.** Anjay wants to buy a car.

____ ____   **5.** Sometimes Anjay's knees hurt.

____ ____   **6.** Anjay decides to visit a friend about his knees.

____ ____   **7.** He takes a taxi to the doctor's office.

____ ____   **8.** The doctor examines his knees for a short time.

____ ____   **9.** Anjay needs to stop riding his bicycle for a while.

____ ____   **10.** The doctor tells Anjay to take the bus.

Underline the word from the story.

1. Anjay rides a (motorcycle/bicycle) everywhere.

2. Anjay doesn't pay for (gas/doctor visits).

3. Anjay is very happy with his (transportation/transfer).

4. Sometimes Anjay's (knees/feet) hurt.

5. Anjay is (happy/worried) about his knees.

6. Anjay needs to stop riding his bicycle for (a year/a while).

7. Anjay needs to (examine/rest) his knees.

8. Anjay doesn't want to buy a (bus/car).

Match the opposites.

_____ **1.** save	**a.** nowhere
_____ **2.** a little	**b.** rest
_____ **3.** everywhere	**c.** a lot
_____ **4.** long	**d.** go
_____ **5.** exercise	**e.** spend
_____ **6.** stop	**f.** short

▪ ▪ ■ Match the words and pictures.

examine	hurt	ride

_____   _____   _____

▪ ▪ ■ Anjay and the Doctor

Practice the dialog with a partner.

Doctor, I'm worried about my knees.

Do they hurt right now?

No, not right now.

When do they hurt?

They hurt when I ride my bicycle. Do you think it's serious?

No, I don't think so.

What can I do?

You need to rest your knees. Stop riding your bicycle for a while.

▌▌▌ Check the correct picture.

1.

_____   _____

2.

_____   _____

3.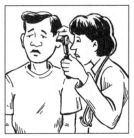

_____   _____

4.

_____   _____

▌▌▌ Check the transportation you use.

Put a check next to the transportation you can use to travel in your city. Write other ideas on the lines below.

____ bicycle   ____ horse

____ car   ____ train

____ walking   ____ scooter

____ helicopter   ____ bus

____ skateboard   ____ motorcycle

_____   _____

▪▪▪ What about you?

Circle *yes* or *no*. Then write questions and ask your partner.

Yes   **No**   **1.** I ride a bicycle everywhere.

Do you ride a bicycle everywhere?

Yes   **No**   **2.** I like riding a bicycle.

_____

Yes   **No**   **3.** I take the bus around my city.

_____

Yes   **No**   **4.** I visit the doctor when I have a problem.

_____

Yes   **No**   **5.** I do what the doctor tells me to do.

_____

▪▪▪ Topics for Discussion or Writing

1. What kind of transportation do people use where you live? What do they use in your native country?

2. How do you get to and from work or school?

3. Do you have a car? What other things do you pay for when you have a car?

Borrow and Lend

Olga sits next to Liza in English class at the adult school. Liza is very nice, but she has one problem. She borrows everything from Olga. Liza doesn't bring paper and a pencil to school. She never brings her book. She brings a cell phone. She brings a hairbrush and makeup. Every day Liza asks Olga for paper, a pencil, a book, and other things for class.

One day Liza says, "I'm thirsty. May I borrow a dollar for a soda?"

"OK," answers Olga. But Olga feels angry.

Then Liza says, "I'm cold. May I borrow your sweater?"

"That's it!" says Olga. "I am tired of lending you everything. You need to bring paper, a pencil, your book, money, and a sweater to school. It is your job to bring these things. You are not a child. You need to take care of yourself!"

"OK," says Liza. "I understand. But Olga, your face is very red. Do you want to borrow my makeup?"

▯▯ Check *yes* or *no.*

Yes   No

____ ____ **1.** Olga sits behind Liza in English class.

____ ____ **2.** Liza borrows everything from Olga.

____ ____ **3.** Liza brings paper and a pencil to school.

____ ____ **4.** Liza brings her book to school.

____ ____ **5.** One day, Liza is thirsty.

____ ____ **6.** Liza wants to borrow a dollar for a soda.

____ ____ **7.** Olga wants to borrow Liza's jacket.

____ ____ **8.** Olga is tired of lending Liza everything.

____ ____ **9.** Liza is a child.

____ ____ **10.** Liza needs to take care of herself.

What is the category?

angry	cold	paper	sweater
book	gloves	pen	thirsty
coat	jacket	pencil	tired

Feelings

1. _____
2. _____
3. _____
4. _____

School Things

1. _____
2. _____
3. _____
4. _____

Warm Clothes

1. _____
2. _____
3. _____
4. _____

Underline the word from the story.

1. Olga sits (next to/near) Liza in English class.

2. She borrows (a few things/everything) from Olga.

3. She never brings her (book/makeup).

4. Liza says, "May I borrow a dollar for a (soda/sandwich)?"

5. Liza wants to borrow a sweater. She is (thirsty/cold).

6. Olga is tired of (lending/sending) things to Liza.

7. Olga says, "You need to take care of (your book/yourself)."

▮▮ ▮ Match the words and pictures.

borrow	lend

_____   _____

▮▮ ▮ Conversation in Class

Practice the dialog with a partner.

May I borrow a pencil?

Sure, you may use this one.

May I borrow your book?

Yes, you may use my book today.

How about a piece of paper?

OK, here you go.

I don't have money for lunch. May I borrow $5?

Sorry, I can't lend you any money.

▌▌▌ Check the correct picture.

1.

_____ _____

2.

_____ _____

3.

_____ _____

4.

_____ _____

▌▌▌ Check the things you borrow or lend.

**Put a check next to the things you borrow or lend.
Write other things on the lines below.**

____ one dollar

____ an English book

____ a piece of paper

____ a toothbrush

____ a car

____ two eggs

____ a lawn mower

____ a CD player

____ a pencil

____ 50 dollars

_____ _____

▎▎▎ What about you?

Circle *yes* or *no.* Then write questions and ask your partner.

Yes   **No**   **1.** I bring a pencil and paper to class.

Do you bring a pencil and paper to class? _____

Yes   **No**   **2.** I bring a book to class.

_____

Yes   **No**   **3.** I bring money to class.

_____

Yes   **No**   **4.** I sometimes borrow things.

_____

Yes   **No**   **5.** I sometimes lend things.

_____

▎▎▎ Topics for Discussion or Writing

1. What are things that you need to bring to school? Do you bring them every day?

2. What other things do you bring to school? Why do you bring them?

3. What are some things you are tired of doing?

The Cell Phone

Pilar is 78 years old. Her granddaughter, Alma, is 29 years old. Pilar likes to go out in the evening. Sometimes she goes out alone. Alma worries about her. Is she hurt? Is she lost? Alma gives Pilar a cell phone. "Here, Grandma," says Alma. "Now I can keep in touch with you."

On Monday evening, Pilar goes to the community center. She is playing bingo with her friends. The cell phone rings. Pilar doesn't answer it. She is looking at her bingo card. The phone rings again. Pilar pushes a button. But it is the wrong button. It rings again and again. Pilar doesn't remember how to answer the cell phone.

Pilar sighs and gets up. She leaves the community center and takes a taxi to Alma's apartment. Pilar knocks on the door. Alma opens it and says, "Oh, Grandma! Are you OK?"

"Yes," answers Pilar. "I'm fine." Pilar gives the cell phone back to Alma. "But I can't keep in touch right now. I want to play bingo."

Check *yes* or *no*.

Yes **No**

____ ____ **1.** Pilar is 78 years old.

____ ____ **2.** She likes to go out in the evening.

____ ____ **3.** Alma worries about her grandfather.

____ ____ **4.** Alma gives Pilar a taxi.

____ ____ **5.** On Tuesday, Pilar goes to the community center.

____ ____ **6.** She is playing bingo with Alma.

____ ____ **7.** Pilar pushes the wrong button on the cell phone.

____ ____ **8.** The phone rings again and again.

____ ____ **9.** Pilar sighs and gets up.

____ ____ **10.** Pilar gives the cell phone back to Alma.

▮▮▮ Complete each sentence.

alone	button	lost	remember
apartment	knocks	playing	worries

1. Pilar likes to go out _____ in the evening.

2. Sometimes her granddaughter _____ about her.

3. Is she hurt? Is she _____?

4. Pilar is fine. She is _____ bingo with her friends.

5. The phone rings, but Pilar pushes the wrong _____.

6. She doesn't _____ how to answer the cell phone.

7. Pilar leaves and takes a taxi to Alma's _____.

8. She _____ on Alma's door to return the phone.

▮▮▮ Match the meanings.

____ **1.** sigh   **a.** a telephone that you carry with you

____ **2.** wrong   **b.** the mother of your mother or father

____ **3.** grandmother   **c.** not correct

____ **4.** hurt   **d.** let out a long, deep breath

____ **5.** cell phone   **e.** return

____ **6.** give back   **f.** injured or in pain

▪▪ ▪ Match the words and pictures.

answer	push a button	ring

_____ _____ _____

▪▪ ▪ Alma and Her Grandmother

Practice the dialog with a partner.

Hi, Grandma! It's Alma. Are you OK?

Hi, Alma. Yes, I'm fine.

Where are you?

I'm at the community center again.

What are you doing?

I'm playing bingo. Can you call me back?

Sure. I can call back in a few minutes.

I have a better idea. Let me call you when I get home.

OK. Good luck at bingo!

▌▌▌ Check the correct picture.

1.
___ ___

3.
___ ___

2.
___ ___

4.
___ ___

▌▌▌ Check the good ideas.

How do you keep in touch with family and friends? Put
a check next to the good ideas. Write other ideas on
the lines below.

____ make phone calls

____ write letters

____ visit them at home

____ read a magazine

____ send e-mail

____ look at photographs

____ send an instant message

____ think about them

____ send a text message

____ meet at a restaurant

_____   _____

▮▮▮ What about you?

Circle *yes* or *no*. Then write questions and ask your partner.

Yes   No   1. I have a cell phone.

Do you have a cell phone?
_____

Yes   No   2. I know how to use a cell phone.

_____

Yes   No   3. I think having a cell phone is a good idea.

_____

Yes   No   4. I worry about my family sometimes.

_____

Yes   No   5. I keep in touch with family and friends.

_____

▮▮▮ Topics for Discussion or Writing

1. Do you go out alone? What do you carry with you when you go out alone?

2. Where do you like to go in the evening? Do you ever get lost?

3. What are some problems you can have with a cell phone?

An Expensive Day

Every summer there is a fair in Beth's city. It is fun for children and adults. The fair has food, games, rides, plants, flowers, and farm animals. This year Beth is taking her son Ryan. Ryan is very excited.

Beth buys two tickets to enter the fair. That's $24. Ryan is hungry. Beth buys two hot dogs and a soda. She pays $9.50. Beth is thirsty. She pays $3.50 for a bottle of water.

Ryan sees a game. It costs $4 to throw a ball into a basket. Ryan plays, but he doesn't win. He wants to play again. Beth opens her purse and pays another $4. He still doesn't win.

Beth looks at her watch. Thirty minutes at the fair and $45 is gone. Ryan points to a ride. "Look!" he says. "That looks fun!" Beth reads the sign: Roller Coaster $7.50.

"Yes, maybe later," says Beth. "Right now it's time for something fun and free. Let's look at the cows."

Check *yes* or *no*.

Yes   No

____ ____   **1.** There is a fair in Beth's city every week.

____ ____   **2.** It's fun for children and adults.

____ ____   **3.** Beth is taking her son this year.

____ ____   **4.** Beth buys three tickets to enter the fair.

____ ____   **5.** Beth pays $24 for two hot dogs and a soda.

____ ____   **6.** She pays $3.50 for a bottle of water.

____ ____   **7.** Ryan plays a game two times.

____ ____   **8.** Ryan wins a stuffed animal.

____ ____   **9.** After 30 minutes, $54 is gone.

____ ____   **10.** Beth wants to do something fun and free.

▮▮▮ What is the category?

bored	cow	goat	pig
bumper cars	excited	horse	roller coaster
carousel	Ferris wheel	hungry	thirsty

Feelings	Farm Animals	Rides
1. _____	1. _____	1. _____
2. _____	2. _____	2. _____
3. _____	3. _____	3. _____
4. _____	4. _____	4. _____

▮▮▮ Match the meanings.

____ 1. purse   a. container for liquids

____ 2. son   b. costing no money

____ 3. free   c. some time in the future

____ 4. enter   d. bag for carrying money

____ 5. later   e. your male child

____ 6. bottle   f. go into

■ ■ Match the words and pictures.

pay	throw	win

_____

_____

_____

■ ■ Buying Fair Tickets

Practice the dialog with a partner.

May I help you?

Yes, two tickets, please.

That's $24.

Does that include the rides?

No, the rides are extra.

How late is the fair open?

It's open until midnight.

Thanks.

Have a good time!

◼︎◼︎◼︎ Write the dollar amount you hear.

1. _____

2. _____

3. _____

4. _____

5. _____

6. _____

7. _____

8. _____

9. _____

10. _____

11. _____

12. _____

◼︎◼︎ Check the things to do.

You want to go to a fair. But you don't want to spend a lot of money. Put a check next to the things you can do. Write other ideas on the lines below.

____ look at the flowers

____ play many games

____ look at farm animals

____ bring water from home

____ forget your purse

____ go on every ride

____ bring food from home

____ look for discount fair tickets

____ sneak in without paying

____ go on only one ride

_____

_____

_____

_____

68 Lesson 11

◼◼◼ What about you?

Circle *yes* or *no.* Then write questions and ask your partner.

Yes   No   1. I go to a fair every summer.

<u>*Do you go to a fair every summer?*</u>

Yes   No   2. I like to see plants and flowers.

_____

Yes   No   3. I like to see farm animals.

_____

Yes   No   4. I like to play games at the fair.

_____

Yes   No   5. I think the fair is very expensive.

_____

◼◼◼ Topics for Discussion or Writing

1. What are some fun places for adults and children in your city? Are they expensive?

2. How much money do you spend at a fair or an amusement park? How do you spend it?

3. What are some free things to do in your city?

A Good Assistant

Ed works for Miss Benson. He is her assistant. He helps in the office. Today is very hot. Miss Benson wants Ed to buy a fan. She is also hungry. She wants Ed to buy her a turkey sandwich.

"Please go right now," says Miss Benson. "There is money in the desk drawer. And don't interrupt me for the next hour. I have an important phone call." She closes her door.

Ed opens the desk drawer. Inside is $20. This is not enough money for a fan and a sandwich. Ed goes out and buys Miss Benson a sandwich. Then he buys a fan. This fan does not use electricity or batteries. It is a small paper fan.

Ed returns to the office. He gives Miss Benson the sandwich and the paper fan. "Sorry," says Ed. "Twenty dollars is very little money."

"That's OK," says Miss Benson. "Ed, you are a good assistant. But you have a lot of work to do. So who will wave the fan while I eat?"

■ ■ Check *yes* or *no*.

Yes   No

____ ____ **1.** Miss Benson works for Ed.

____ ____ **2.** Miss Benson wants Ed to buy a fan.

____ ____ **3.** She also wants a tuna sandwich.

____ ____ **4.** There is money in the desk drawer.

____ ____ **5.** Miss Benson wants Ed to interrupt.

____ ____ **6.** She has an important phone call.

____ ____ **7.** There is $200 inside the desk drawer.

____ ____ **8.** Ed buys a fan that uses electricity.

____ ____ **9.** Miss Benson is angry.

____ ____ **10.** Miss Benson wants someone to wave the fan while she eats.

▎▎◼ Underline the word from the story.

1. Ed is Miss Benson's (administrator/assistant).

2. Miss Benson is hot and (angry/hungry).

3. There is money in a (purse/drawer).

4. She says, "Don't interrupt me for the next (hour/day)."

5. She has an important (visitor/phone call).

6. Twenty dollars is (not enough/too much) money for
a fan and a sandwich.

7. Ed buys a fan that does not use (paper/batteries).

8. Miss Benson says, "Who will wave the fan while
I (eat/sleep)?"

▎▎◼ Match the meanings.

_____ **1.** interrupt

_____ **2.** drawer

_____ **3.** assistant

_____ **4.** electricity

_____ **5.** hour

_____ **6.** sandwich

a. 60 minutes

b. a person who helps another at work

c. a box that slides in and out of a
piece of furniture

d. power carried by wires

e. stop or break in on

f. two pieces of bread with food
between them

■ ■ ■ Complete the story.

assistant	fan	office	paper
desk	important	only	sandwich

Miss Benson has a good _____. His name is Ed. Ed

helps her in the _____. Today Miss Benson wants a turkey

_____. She also wants a _____. Miss Benson

says there is money in the _____ drawer.

Then she closes her office door. She has an _____

phone call. Ed finds _____ $20 in the drawer. He comes

back with a sandwich and a small _____ fan. Twenty

dollars is very little money.

■ ■ ■ Finding a Fan

Practice the dialog with a partner.

How much is that electric fan?

That one is on sale for $33.95.

How about the one that uses batteries?

It's a little less. It's 16.95.

Do you have anything cheaper?

You can buy a paper fan for about $5.

Check the correct picture.

1.
____   ____

2.
____   ____

3.
____   ____

4.
____   ____

Check the things you buy.

You are Miss Benson's assistant. She wants everything on the list below. There is only $50 in the desk drawer. Put a check next to the things you buy.

____ a sandwich   ____ paper for the printer

____ an electric fan   ____ a bottle of water

____ a computer   ____ a file cabinet

____ a cookie   ____ a clock

____ 100 stamps   ____ an answering machine

▪▪ What about you?

Circle *yes* or *no*. Then write questions and ask your partner.

Yes   No   1. I work for another person.

Do you work for another person?

Yes   No   2. I think Ed is a good assistant.

Yes   No   3. I like turkey sandwiches.

Yes   No   4. I have a fan that uses electricity.

Yes   No   5. I have a paper fan.

▪▪ Topics for Discussion or Writing

1. What things can help you feel better when it's hot? Do you have a fan? Do you have an air conditioner?

2. What do you usually eat for lunch? If you eat out, how much do you spend?

3. When is it OK to interrupt someone? When is it not OK?

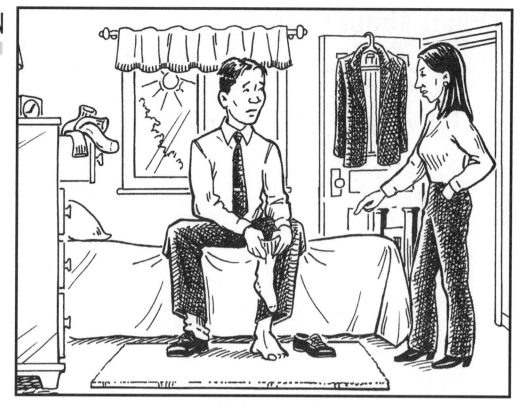

White Socks

Jack always wears white socks. He likes white socks and doesn't like other colors. Jack wears white socks Monday, Tuesday, Wednesday, Thursday, Friday, Saturday, and Sunday. He wears them morning, afternoon, and evening. He wears white socks at work. He wears white socks at home.

Jack's wife, Susie, is tired of his white socks. "Jack," she says. "You need more variety. Let's go shopping."

Jack and Susie go to the department store. Susie picks up three different pairs of socks. They are blue, brown, and black.

Susie thinks these socks are nice. They match Jack's other clothes.

"How about these?" asks Susie. Jack feels the socks. They are soft. They are the right length. And they are not too expensive.

"These are great," says Jack. "Let's buy them." Susie is very happy. Jack sees a sales clerk. "Excuse me," he says. "I'd like to buy these socks, but not in these colors. Do you have them in white?"

■ ■ ■ Check *yes* or *no*.

Yes   No

____ ____ **1.** Jack always wears white socks.

____ ____ **2.** Jack likes other colors of socks.

____ ____ **3.** Jack wears black socks at work.

____ ____ **4.** Susie likes Jack's white socks.

____ ____ **5.** Jack and Susie go to the department store.

____ ____ **6.** Susie picks up one pair of socks.

____ ____ **7.** The socks are blue, brown, and black.

____ ____ **8.** The socks are soft.

____ ____ **9.** The socks are very expensive.

____ ____ **10.** Jack wants to buy the socks in white.

What is the category?

afternoon	brown	morning	Thursday
black	evening	night	Tuesday
blue	Monday	Sunday	white

Times of Day

1. _____

2. _____

3. _____

4. _____

Colors

1. _____

2. _____

3. _____

4. _____

Days of the Week

1. _____

2. _____

3. _____

4. _____

Match the meanings.

____ **1.** wife

____ **2.** pair

____ **3.** length

____ **4.** socks

____ **5.** match

____ **6.** variety

a. to go well together

b. set of two

c. different types of things

d. how long something is

e. clothes you wear on your feet

f. married woman

▮▮▮ Complete the story.

afternoon	husband	Saturday	tired
department	length	shopping	Wednesday

Susie's _____ likes to wear white socks. He wears

them Monday, Tuesday, _____, Thursday, Friday,

_____, and Sunday. He wears them morning,

_____, and evening.

Susie is _____ of his white socks. Susie says, "Let's go

_____." Susie and Jack go to the _____ store.

Susie finds soft socks that are the right _____. Jack likes

them. But he wants to buy them in white.

▮▮▮ More White Socks

Practice the dialog with a partner.

May I help you?

Sure. Do you have these socks in white?

Yes, we do.

Great. I'd like to buy them.

How many pairs?

I'll take three pairs.

Check the correct picture.

1.
_____ _____

3.
_____ _____

2.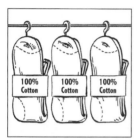
_____ _____

4.
_____ _____

Check the colors.

Put a check next to the colors you like to wear. Write some other colors on the lines below.

____ blue	____ gray	____ red
____ green	____ yellow	____ purple
____ white	____ silver	____ brown
____ pink	____ aqua	____ gold
____ black	____ orange	____ beige

_____ _____ _____

80 Lesson 13

■ ■ What about you?

Circle *yes* or *no*. Then write questions and ask your partner.

Yes   No   1. I like white socks.

Do you like white socks? _____

Yes   No   2. I have different colors of socks.

_____

Yes   No   3. I think Jack needs more variety.

_____

Yes   No   4. I am tired of some of my clothes.

_____

Yes   No   5. I like shopping for clothes.

_____

■ ■ Topics for Discussion or Writing

1. Where do you like to shop? What are the names of some stores in your city?

2. How often do you go shopping for clothes?

3. What do you wear at home? What do you wear at work? Are some clothes the same?

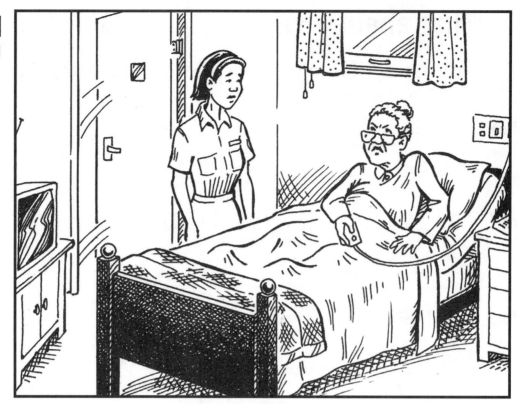

A Call for Help

Chan works in a retirement home. She helps take care of the elderly people living there. Chan likes most of the people very much. But Mrs. Stevens is a difficult person. She is healthy and strong, but always calls for help. She feels too hot or too cold. Her room is too dark or too light. She wants her curtain opened or closed.

Chan hears the bell. It is Mrs. Stevens. Chan goes to her room and asks, "What can I do for you?"

Mrs. Stevens says, "I am not comfortable in this bed. My feet are too high and my head is too low." Chan pushes a button and adjusts the bed.

Then Mrs. Stevens says, "I can't see the TV." Chan moves the TV to the right. "Now move it to the left," says Mrs. Stevens.

Chan tells Mrs. Stevens that she needs to go now. Other people need help, too. Mr. Ramirez needs his medicine. Mrs. Finch needs her dinner. "Go ahead," says Mrs. Stevens. "But don't help too much. They need to be independent."

Check *yes* or *no.*

Yes	No	
____	____	**1.** Chan works in a retirement home.
____	____	**2.** She takes care of young people.
____	____	**3.** Mrs. Stevens always calls for help.
____	____	**4.** Mrs. Stevens is unhealthy and weak.
____	____	**5.** Mrs. Stevens is comfortable in her bed.
____	____	**6.** Her feet are too high and her head is too low.
____	____	**7.** Chan pushes a button and adjusts the bed.
____	____	**8.** Mrs. Stevens can see the TV.
____	____	**9.** Other people need help, too.
____	____	**10.** Mrs. Finch needs her curtain opened.

Underline the word from the story.

1. Chan (lives/works) in a retirement home.

2. Chan likes most of the (guests/people) very much.

3. Mrs. Stevens is a (difficult/helpful) person.

4. Her room is too dark or too (low/light).

5. She wants her curtain opened or (closed/cold).

6. Chan hears the (yell/bell).

7. Chan pushes a button and adjusts the (TV/bed).

8. Mr. Ramirez needs his (medicine/meal).

Match the opposites.

_____ 1. opened   **a.** low

_____ 2. dark   **b.** light

_____ 3. left   **c.** closed

_____ 4. strong   **d.** weak

_____ 5. hot   **e.** cold

_____ 6. high   **f.** right

Match the words and pictures.

hear a bell	help someone

_____   _____

Helping Mrs. Stevens

Practice the dialog with a partner.

Did you call me, Mrs. Stevens?

Yes. Please come here, Chan. I need help.

What can I do for you?

I can't see the TV.

Let me move it to the right.

No, that's too far.

Sorry. I can move it to the left. How is that?

It's OK now. But I don't like this program.

Check the correct picture.

1.
_____ _____

3.
_____ _____

2.
_____ _____

4.
_____ _____

Check the things you do.

Put a check next to the things you do independently. Write some things you need help with on the lines below.

_____ turn on a light

_____ fix a leaky faucet

_____ open a curtain

_____ cook dinner

_____ study English

_____ paint a house

_____ change a car tire

_____ carry something heavy

_____ change the channel on the TV

_____ use a computer

_____ _____

▮▮ What about you?

Circle *yes* or *no*. Then write questions and ask your partner.

Yes   No   1. I work in a retirement home.

Do you work in a retirement home?

Yes   No   2. I take care of an elderly person.

_____

Yes   No   3. I like the people where I work.

_____

Yes   No   4. I know a difficult person.

_____

Yes   No   5. I need to be more independent.

_____

▮▮ Topics for Discussion or Writing

1. Is your home always comfortable? Is it sometimes too dark, too light, too hot, or too cold? What can you do to make your home more comfortable?

2. Who can come if you need help? How do you get help?

3. In what ways do you need to be more independent?

Graduation Party

Marta's daughter Silvia is graduating from high school this afternoon. Marta is very proud. After the graduation ceremony, she is having a big party for Silvia. Many people are coming: grandparents, uncles, aunts, cousins, friends, and neighbors. Marta is expecting 75 people at her home tonight.

Marta is working hard to get ready for the party. She is making lasagna and salad. Silvia is sleeping. After that, Marta is cleaning the bathroom. Silvia is talking on the phone. Then Marta is dusting the furniture and vacuuming the carpet. Silvia is taking a shower and singing.

Twenty minutes later, Marta looks in the bathroom. Silvia is not there, but her dirty clothes and towel are on the floor. The room is a mess. Marta is very angry. "Silvia," calls Marta. "I have a graduation present for you."

Silvia opens her bedroom door. She is excited. "What is it?" she asks.

"It's a mess in the bathroom," answers Marta. "Please be more considerate. Clean it up right now. Then help me make a cake for your party."

Check *yes* or *no.*

Yes   No

____ ____ **1.** Silvia is graduating from elementary school.

____ ____ **2.** After the ceremony, there is a big party for Silvia.

____ ____ **3.** Marta is expecting 35 people at her home tonight.

____ ____ **4.** Silvia is working hard.

____ ____ **5.** Marta is making lasagna and salad.

____ ____ **6.** Silvia is dusting the furniture and vacuuming the carpet.

____ ____ **7.** Silvia is taking a shower and singing.

____ ____ **8.** The bathroom is a mess.

____ ____ **9.** Silvia needs to clean up the bathroom right now.

What is the category?

anniversary	cleaning	dusting	uncle
aunt	cooking	graduation	vacuuming
birthday	cousin	grandparent	wedding

Housework	Family Members	Reasons for a Party
1. _____	1. _____	1. _____
2. _____	2. _____	2. _____
3. _____	3. _____	3. _____
4. _____	4. _____	4. _____

Match the meanings.

_____ **1.** considerate

_____ **2.** furniture

_____ **3.** party

_____ **4.** mess

_____ **5.** lasagna

_____ **6.** bathroom

a. room with a sink, toilet, and shower

b. people celebrating together

c. things such as tables and chairs

d. clutter or disorder

e. thinking about people's feelings

f. baked pasta dish

▮▮▮ Complete the story.

angry	considerate	high school	shower
ceremony	hard	proud	vacuuming

Silvia is graduating from _____. Her mother is very

_____. After the _____ there is a party.

Silvia's mother, Marta, is working _____. She is cooking

and cleaning. She is dusting and _____.

Silvia is not working hard. She is sleeping. Later, after

she takes a _____, the bathroom is a mess. Marta is

_____. She tells Silvia to be more _____.

▮▮▮ Asking for Help

Practice the dialog with a partner.

May I talk to you for a minute?

Sure. What is it?

The bathroom is a mess. Please clean it up.

Sorry, I'll be off the phone in 10 minutes.

No, clean it up right now. Then help me in
the kitchen.

OK, Mom. I'm coming.

■ ■ ■ Check the correct picture.

1.
_____ _____

3.
_____ _____

2.
_____ _____

4.
_____ _____

■ ■ Check the things you do.

Put a check next to the things you do at home. Write other housework you do on the lines below.

_____ cook meals

_____ do laundry

_____ clean the bathroom

_____ make the bed

_____ vacuum the carpet

_____ dust the furniture

_____ sweep the floor

_____ take out the trash

_____ pick up things

_____ wash the dishes

_____ _____

What about you?

Circle *yes* or *no.* Then write questions and ask your partner.

Yes   No   1. I have parties for people in my family.

Do you have parties for people in your family?

Yes   No   2. Many people come to my home.

_____

Yes   No   3. I work hard cooking and cleaning.

_____

Yes   No   4. I like to cook for a lot of people.

_____

Yes   No   5. I get angry when my house is a mess.

_____

Topics for Discussion or Writing

1. Do you have parties at home? What do you like to cook?

2. What kind of messes do you have at home? Who cleans them up?

3. What do you think is a good graduation gift? What other gifts do you like to give?

Listening Exercise Prompts

■ Lesson 1

Check the correct picture. (page 8)

1. He is having lunch alone.
2. The man is leaving the restaurant.
3. There is something on the floor.
4. He is giving the woman her wallet.

■ Lesson 2

Check the correct picture. (page 14)

1. She is looking at her watch.
2. There is an e-mail message from Aunt Clara.
3. Her sister is probably sleeping.
4. Look for a travel agent.

■ Lesson 3

Check the correct picture. (page 20)

1. My friend doesn't like rainy weather.
2. He lives in the city.
3. I am taking T-shirts, shorts, and sandals.
4. Pack an umbrella for your trip.

■ Lesson 4

Check the correct picture. (page 26)

1. The waiter comes to take their order.
2. This food is extra hot.
3. They are trading plates.
4. She is drinking all of her water.

■ Lesson 5

Write the dollar amount you hear. (page 32)

1. Your fine is $500.
2. Do I have to pay $95?
3. This ticket is for $180.
4. You need to pay $30.
5. The fee is $385.
6. He has to pay $115 for that.
7. Are you sure I have to pay $140?
8. Yes, the ticket is $65.
9. Parking there will cost you $45.
10. She needs to pay $70.
11. Can you believe I have to pay $154?
12. That can cost you $400.

■ Lesson 6

Check the correct picture. (page 38)

1. He likes big parties and dancing.
2. She is upset.
3. That music is too loud.
4. You need to find another place to live.

■ Lesson 7

Check the correct picture. (page 44)

1. He is making a call.
2. You can get your hair done at the hotel salon.
3. She is eating lunch at the Garden Restaurant.
4. Write down the message so you can remember it.

Write the time you hear. (page 44)

1. Call the front desk at 3:00.
2. Are we having lunch at 1:00?
3. The hotel salon is open at 10:00.
4. The zoo closes at 6:00.
5. You can get breakfast at 7:00.
6. I start work at 5:00.
7. Please deliver this message at 11:00.
8. This restaurant doesn't serve dinner after 9:00.
9. My husband is resting until 2:00.
10. Do you go home at 4:00?
11. Can you give them a call at 8:00?
12. The restaurant opens at 12:00.

■ Lesson 8

Check the correct picture. (page 50)

1. He likes riding a bicycle.
2. He is saving money.
3. The doctor examines his knees for a long time.
4. You need to rest your knees.

■ Lesson 9

Check the correct picture. (page 56)

1. May I borrow your pencil?
2. She brings makeup to school.
3. She wants to borrow a dollar for a soda.
4. I'm cold. May I borrow your sweater?

■ Lesson 10

Check the correct picture. (page 62)

1. My grandmother is 78 years old.
2. That woman is hurt.
3. She is taking a taxi.
4. She is giving back the cell phone.

■ Lesson 11

Write the dollar amount you hear. (page 68)

1. One admission ticket is $12.
2. The water comes to $3.50.
3. The Ferris wheel costs $6.

4. May I please have $4 for ice cream?
5. A small cotton candy is $2.75.
6. A ticket for the bumper cars is $5.
7. Two hot dogs and a soda is $9.50.
8. That's $15 for your carousel tickets.
9. I need $8 to play the game twice.
10. It costs $7.50 to ride the roller coaster.
11. The popcorn is only $1.50.
12. Our family spent $110 at the fair.

Lesson 12

Check the correct picture. (page 74)

1. Today is very hot.
2. He opens the desk drawer.
3. He can buy her a small paper fan.
4. Please wave the fan while I eat.

Lesson 13

Check the correct picture. (page 80)

1. He wears white socks at home.
2. She picks up three different pairs of socks.
3. These socks are soft.
4. He sees a sales clerk.

Lesson 14

Check the correct picture. (page 86)

1. She is healthy and strong.
2. This curtain is closed.
3. My head is too low.
4. I need to take Mrs. Finch her dinner.

Lesson 15

Check the correct picture. (page 92)

1. Help me make a cake for your party.
2. She is taking a shower.
3. You need to vacuum the carpet.
4. She is sleeping.